D1615011

Drama for Stude
Volume 3

Staff

Editorial: David M. Galens, *Editor*. Terry Browne, Christopher Busiel, Clare Cross, Tom Faulkner, John Fiero, David M. Galens, Carole Hamilton, Sheri Metzger, Daniel Moran, Terry Nienhuis, William P. Wiles, Joanne Woolway, Etta Worthington, *Entry Writers*. Elizabeth Cranston, Kathleen J. Edgar, Jennifer Gariepy, Dwayne D. Hayes, Kurt Kuban, Joshua Kondek, Tom Ligotti, Scot Peacock, Patti Tippett, Pam Zuber, *Contributing Editors*. James Draper, *Managing Editor*. Diane Telgen, *"For Students" Line Coordinator*. Jeffery Chapman, *Programmer/Analyst*.

Research: Victoria B. Cariappa, *Research Team Manager*. Andy Malonis, Barb McNeil, *Research Specialists*. Julia C. Daniel, Tamara C. Nott, Tracie A. Richardson, Cheryl L. Warnock, *Research Associates*. Phyllis P. Blackman, Jeffrey D. Daniels,

Corrine A. Stocker, *Research Assistants*.

Permissions: Susan M. Trosky, *Permissions Manager*. Kimberly F. Smilay, *Permissions Specialist*. Steve Cusack and Kelly A. Quin, *Permissions Associates*.

Production: Mary Beth Trimper, *Production Director*. Evi Seoud, *Assistant Production Manager*. Shanna Heilveil, *Production Assistant*.

Graphic Services: Randy Bassett, *Image Database Supervisor*. Robert Duncan and Michael Logusz, *Imaging Specialists*. Pamela A. Reed, *Photography Coordinator*. Gary Leach, *Macintosh Artist*.

Product Design: Cynthia Baldwin, *Product Design Manager*. Cover Design: Michelle DiMercurio, *Art Director*. Page Design: Pamela A. E. Galbreath, *Senior Art Director*.

Copyright Notice

editors or publisher. Errors brought to the attention of the publisher and verified to the satisfaction of the publisher will be corrected in future editions.

This publication is a creative work fully protected by all applicable copyright laws, as well as by misappropriation, trade secret, unfair competition, and other applicable laws. The authors and editors of this work have added value to the underlying factual material herein through one or more of the following: unique and original selection, coordination, expression, arrangement, and classification of information. All rights to this publication will be vigorously defended.

Waiting for Lefty

Clifford Odets

1935

Introduction

Clifford Odets's *Waiting for Lefty* is a vigorous, confrontational work, based on a 1934 strike of unionized New York cabdrivers. Explicit political messages dominate the play, whose ultimate goal was nothing less than the promotion of a communist revolution in America. Appearing at the height of the Great Depression, the play's original 1935 production was a critical and popular sensation. *Waiting for Lefty* was widely staged throughout the country and brought Odets sudden fame. While its dramatic style has long since fallen out of fashion (along with the idealistic politics that inspired it), it is considered a prime example of a *genre* known as "revolutionary" or "agitprop" theatre. (The latter term is a combination of "agitation" and "propaganda.") The idealistic practitioners of agitprop sought to harness the power of drama to a specific political cause and create a "people's theatre" for the new world that would follow the revolution.

A one-act play in eight episodes, *Waiting for Lefty* is composed of two basic stagings. The main setting is a union hall, where the members wait to take a hotly-contested strike vote. While the corrupt union leader Harry Fatt arrogantly tries to discourage the members from walking out, support for a strike is high, and the workers nervously await the arrival of the leader of the strike faction, Lefty Costello. As they wait, members of the strike committee address the workers, each telling the story of how he came to be involved in the union and convinced of the necessity for a strike. These individual stories are sketched in a series of vignettes, played out in a small spotlit area of the stage. Each is a story of unjust victimization, mirroring Fatt's heavy-handed attempts to control the union meeting. The building tension and emotion reaches a climax when the news arrives that Lefty has been murdered, and the meeting erupts in a unanimous demand to "Strike! Strike!"

Modern audiences may find *Waiting for Lefty's*

style and dogmatic politics strange and unfamiliar; it is rarely produced and is often characterized as an historical curiosity. More than most dramas, it is the product of a particular time and place—for its overriding concern was to influence that time and place, not to create "immortal art," and certainly not to create diverting, light-hearted entertainment. It faced its grim times squarely and offered its audience a stirring vision of hope. In this sense *Waiting for Lefty* is seen as an important dramatic work that offers historical evidence of the social power and aspirations of theatre.

Author Biography

Clifford Odets is best-known for his early, Depression-era dramas, particularly *Waiting for Lefty*, an overt work of propaganda that tells a story of working-class struggle, intended to promote a socialist revolution. His later works were more conventional in style and content and seldom preached a political message. Though his later work often met with critical and commercial approval, he never regained the prominence he enjoyed in the 1930s. He is primarily associated with the left-wing "agitprop" (a term defined as political propaganda as proffered through literature, drama, art, and music) theatre of that time.

Odets was born July 18, 1906, in Philadelphia, Pennsylvania, the son of Russian Jewish immigrants. He moved with his family to the Bronx at the age of six. Though he would associate himself with the political causes of the working-class and downtrodden, his early circumstances were decidedly middle-class. Odets rebelled against his father's strong wish that he enter the family printing business, aspiring instead to become an actor. He dropped out of high school in 1923 and entered into a succession of minor jobs in the theatrical world, eventually finding his way to the Group Theater in 1930.

As its name suggests, the Group Theater was a collective, whose members embraced socialist principles and saw their theatrical work as an expression of their political values. Disdaining the "star-system" and commercialism of Broadway, their ideal was to be a community of equals, working selflessly together to produce works that would serve to help transform society itself by dramatizing the political realities of the times and inspiring audiences to join the struggle for change. Odets was asked to submit plays for the troupe, and the productions of his work began to attract wide critical attention. When *Waiting for Lefty* debuted in 1935, it proved immensely popular and drew high praise from drama critics, securing for its author a sudden, national reputation. The play won both the Yale Drama Prize and the New Theatre League award for 1935 and was widely produced across the country.

Odets began receiving offers from Hollywood and from the "big-time," mainstream (Broadway) theatres and production companies. Though he continued to work with the Group Theater, he also pursued these more commercial opportunities, with the justification that the income they produced would subsidize the continuing efforts of the Group. In 1937 he wrote *Golden Boy*, the tale of a troubled prizefighter; it became his greatest commercial success, and the sale of the movie rights for $75,000 provided much-needed capital for the collective. Like most of Odets's subsequent work, its style is more conventional than that of *Waiting for Lefty*, and it lacks an overt political message. As Odets rose to prominence and mainstream approval, many left-wing contemporaries accused him of "selling out," abandoning his principles to enhance the commercial appeal of his work. Eventually he broke with the Group Theatre and the agitprop style.

Odets became a Hollywood screenwriter and continued to write for the theatre. In 1952 he was called before a Congressional subcommittee investigating "un-American activities" and asked to testify about his previous left-wing agitation efforts. This experience, part of the infamous anti-communist "witch hunts" of the McCarthy era (named for Senator Joseph McCarthy, who spearheaded the persecution), appears to have had a devastating impact on Odets. He had already renounced many of his earlier political beliefs, but his very association with left-wing causes left him vulnerable to being "blacklisted" (prohibited from working) as a "security risk." Many people in his position were forced to either abandon their careers or testify against their former associates—who would then become targets of the same sort of persecution.

While Odets did not technically "name names" in his subcommittee appearance (each of the people he mentioned had already come to the attention of the committee), he did cooperate enough to remove himself from further suspicion. He later expressed guilt and "repulsion" for his testimony and apparently was tormented by the matter for the rest of his life. He continued to write screenplays, teleplays, and dramas but his production dropped off after 1952, and he never regained his earlier prominence. He was honored with an Award of

Merit Medal from the American Academy of Arts and Letters in 1961. Odets died two years later on August 14, 1963, in Los Angeles, California.

Prologue: The Strike Meeting

The curtain rises on a union meeting, already in progress. Harry Fatt, the union leader, is addressing a group of workers seated before him. A six-or seven-man committee sits in a semicircle behind him. Fatt speaks forcefully against a proposed strike, noting the failure of several recent strikes, and arguing that such tactics are both unproductive and unnecessary. He expresses confidence that the President is "looking out for our interests," and suggests that those who wish to strike are communists ("reds"), out to destroy everything Americans hold dear. Despite his confidence and heated rhetoric, Fatt's message is not well-received. Throughout his speech the voices of workers rise in opposition and defiance, while the ominous presence of a "gunman," who menaces the hecklers, suggests that Fatt's leadership has less than honest democratic origins.

From the workers comes an enthusiastic call for Lefty, the (elected) chairman of the strike committee, who is mysteriously absent from the meeting. Fatt suggests that Lefty has abandoned the workers. The workers demand to hear from the other members of the strike committee. Unable to calm the crowd, Fatt "insolently" gives way to Joe Mitchell, a committee member. Joe denies that he is a "red," offering his war wounds as evidence of his patriotism, and defends Lefty's courage and conviction. He speaks to the workers of their own poverty and exploitation, arguing that a strike is the only way they might achieve "a living wage." Joe tells the workers they must each make up their own minds on the issue; as for himself, "[m]y wife made up my mind last week." As he begins to relate the experience, the stage lights fade out.

Scene I: Joe and Edna

A spotlight creates a small playing space within the meeting; the workers remain "dimly visible in the outer dark," occasionally commenting on the action. Joe, a cabdriver, comes home from a long and unprofitable day's work to a desperate household. The furniture has just been repossessed, the rent is two months past due, the children have gone to bed without dinner, and his wife, Edna, is in a sullen and bitter mood. Exasperated by their poverty, Edna taunts and challenges Joe, finally threatening to leave him for her old boyfriend, Bud Haas.

Edna makes it clear that she doesn't directly blame Joe for their condition but rather the bosses who set the terms of his employment. She resents her husband for passively accepting his lot. "For God's sake, do something, Joe," Edna pleads, "get wise. Maybe get your buddies together, maybe go on strike for better money." Joe first argues that "strikes don't work" but later admits that the union leaders are "racketeers" who rule by force without consulting the workers—standing up to them could cost his life. Edna replies that she'd rather see him dead if he won't fight for his family. Once more she urges him to take action by helping organize the union cabbies to" [s]weep out those racketeers," to "stand up like men and fight for the crying kids and wives." This time, her argument wins Joe over; he jumps up, kisses her passionately, and rushes out to find Lefty (who apparently has already begun organizing within the union). As Edna stands in triumph, the stage lights come up and the scene returns to the union meeting, where Joe concludes his speech by calling for a strike.

Continuing the workers' stories, Miller is called upon to relate the circumstances that brought him to the strike meeting.

Scene II: Lab Assistant Episode

After a blackout, the scene finds Miller, a lab assistant, in the luxurious office of his employer, the industrialist Fayette. Fayette compliments Miller's work, gives him a twenty-dollar raise, and tells him he's being transferred to a new project working under a "very important chemist," Dr. Brenner. Miller's gratitude for the promotion gradually dissolves as the particulars of the project are revealed. He will have to live at the lab full-time throughout the project, working in utmost secrecy. His job will be to develop chemical weapons for the military in preparation for the "new war" Fayette considers imminent. Having lost a brother and two cousins in the last war, Miller expresses reservations about the nature of the work. Fayette appeals to Miller's self-interest: the project will mean advancement in his career and personal exemption from military service. Fayette believes that the consequences of the work are "not our worry," and that business can never be "sentimental over human life." Finally, he asks Miller to provide him with "confidential" reports on Brenner throughout the project—to, in effect, spy on his colleague. Miller refuses indignantly, saying that he's "not built that way." Fayette offers a larger raise, appeals to Miller's patriotism, and eventually threatens to fire him, all to no avail: Miller stands firm in his decision, is fired by Fayette, and concludes the interview by punching his (former) boss "square in the mouth."

Scene III: The Young Hack and His Girl

In another domestic scene, Florrie and her brother Irv argue about her boyfriend, Sid, who is coming to take her out dancing. She and Sid are in love and want to marry. But like Joe, Sid is a cabdriver and doesn't earn enough to support a family. Moreover, Florrie and Irv's mother is bedridden, and the family has been struggling. They depend on her for the care and housework she provides as well as the income from her job as a store clerk. Irv recognizes that Sid is serious in his intentions but intentions aren't enough: Florrie's duty is to her family and it's simply "no time to get married." Irv demands that she stop seeing Sid and even threatens to beat the boyfriend up. While she asserts the right to a life of her own, she agrees that she and Sid need to have a serious talk.

Sid arrives, and the lovers soon begin to confront their situation together. Despite their love, they can find no way around the economic facts. They've been engaged for three years now, but Sid is no closer to being able to provide for her and sees no prospects for the future. His brother Sam, despite the advantage of a college education, has just joined the navy because he was unable to find a job. Sid feels like "a dog," unable to "look the world straight in the face, spit in its eye like a man should do"—though perhaps, with Florrie beside him, he might. "But something wants us to be lonely like that," she answers, "crawling alone in the dark. Or they want us trapped." Sid identifies that "something" as "the big-shot money men" in power, who keep people like themselves in poverty and send people like Sam off to war. Reluctantly, he concludes that they must separate ("If we can't climb higher than this together—we better stay apart.") After a last, passionate dance to a phonograph record, he tries to leave but is unable. Florrie bursts into tears, Sid falls to his knees and buries his face in her lap. The scene blacks out.

Scene IV: Labor Spy Episode

The action returns to the union meeting. Fatt argues once again that a strike won't succeed. He introduces a speaker with "practical strike experience" to help persuade the workers of that fact: Tom Clayton from Philadelphia, the veteran of a failed taxi strike some three months ago. This "thin, modest individual" tells his fellow-cabbies that Fatt is right, but he is soon shouted down by a "Clear Voice" in the crowd who claims that "Clayton" is an impostor, a company spy named Clancy. Over Fatt's objections, the Voice details Clancy's long career as a strike-breaker. Fatt demands proof, and "Clayton" calls his accuser a liar, claiming never to have seen him before. At this point the "voice" identifies himself—as the traitor's own brother. As the impostor "Clayton" flees down the center aisle, Fatt pretends to have been ignorant of the deception.

Scene V: The Young Actor

An unemployed actor named Philips waits in the office of a theatrical producer, Grady, making conversation with Grady's secretary—who is clearly not an admirer of her boss. She reveals that Grady is luxuriating in a perfumed bath while he makes Philips wait. She advises Philips to lie about his experience, since Grady "wouldn't know a good actor if he fell over him in the dark." Philips confides to her that he is desperate for a job. She offers him a dollar. He answers that it won't help much: his wife is expecting their first child in a month, and he must find a way to support them.

Grady (played by Fatt) enters, asks his secretary to call the hospital to "see how Boris is," and conducts a gruff job interview. He soon catches Philips in a lie about his resume and abruptly decides he can't use the actor; he has an opening for the part of a soldier and needs a bigger man. Philips protests that he has military experience and is sure he can act the role. He guarantees a fine performance, telling the producer that he's an "artist." But Grady is a businessman with investments to protect, and the safe course is to cast for physical type, not to take chances on unknown actors. "What do I care if you can act it?," he asks Philips, "Your face and height we want, not your soul, son." Philips pleads for any work, however small, but Grady has nothing to offer. As he concludes the interview, the secretary reports that "Boris" is doing fine.

After Grady leaves, the secretary tells Philips that "Boris" is Grady's dog, in the hospital to be castrated. "They do the same to you, but you don't know it!," she says, then advises, "In the next office, don't let them see you down in the mouth." As he starts to leave, thanking her for treating him "like a human being," she offers the dollar again, telling him it will buy him ten loaves of bread—or nine loaves and "one copy of The Communist Manifesto." "What's that?," he asks, taking the dollar; she promises to give him a copy, describing the document, in biblical terms, as the revelation of "a new earth and a new heaven" and of a world where the *militant*, not the meek, will inherit the earth. "Come out in the light, Comrade," she says, as the scene dissolves in blackout.

Scene VI: Intern Episode

Dr. Barnes, an elderly hospital administrator, angrily finishes a phone call, referring to a decision he had opposed involving a Dr. Benjamin. He is about to pour himself a drink when Benjamin arrives at his office. Hiding the bottle, he invites the young doctor into his office. Benjamin reports that he has just been replaced on one of his "charity cases" by an incompetent surgeon who happens to be a Senator's nephew; the case is serious, and he fears the patient's life is in danger. Barnes tries to evade the issue but soon lets down his guard: "God damn it, do you think it's my fault?," he despairs. Benjamin apologetically starts to leave, but Barnes calls him back.

Gradually, Barnes reveals that the hospital will be undergoing several changes—decisions he has fought against and is ashamed to carry out. Because of budget cutbacks, a charity ward is being closed and several staff members will be laid off. Benjamin has shown great promise and is considered "top man here"—yet he is to lose his job while less qualified doctors keep theirs. Barnes confirms that Benjamin is a victim of anti-Semitism, despite the presence of several wealthy Jews on the hospital's board of directors. He remarks that he sees little difference "between wealthy Jews and rich Gentiles" and bitterly complains that "doctors don't run medicine" in this "rich man's country."

A phone call interrupts Barnes with the news that Benjamin's patient has died on the operating table; it is the emotional "last straw" for both men. Benjamin had doubted radical political doctrines before but now sees them confirmed by his experience: "you don't believe theories until they happen to you." Barnes encourages his colleague's outrage and new-found determination. He is too old for the cause (a "fossil" who must yet provide for an invalid daughter), but he exhorts the younger man to fight the system that has victimized him. Benjamin considers emigrating to Russia for "the wonderful opportunity to do good work in their socialized medicine," but he chooses instead to stay and work for change in America. He will find a working-class job ("maybe drive a cab") and join the proletarian struggle. He raises high a clenched fist as the scene blacks out.

Conclusion: Strike Meeting

Back at the union meeting, an old worker named Agate Keller offers a rambling speech. He seems eccentric and suggests that he "ain't been right" since falling out of the cradle in infancy. Yet Keller also shows a passionate attachment to the working-class cause. As an eleven-year-old factory worker, he lost an eye in an industrial accident; he mentions that there was a union in that factory but that its officers were corrupt and did nothing for the members. Fatt and his supporters object loudly, but Keller demurs that he was merely speaking of "unions in general" and expresses confidence that "our officers is all aces."

Keller goes on to tell about being unable to wear his union button today: it seems that, when he reached for his coat, he found the button was on fire —"blush[ing] itself to death," out of shame. Fatt again tries to shout him down and the gunman approaches menacingly, but Keller breaks away and continues. A group of workers forms protectively around him, and, with rising emotion, he declares that their lives are on the line, that the choice is between "slow death and war." "What are we waiting for?," he cries. "Don't wait for Lefty! He might never come." A worker breaks in with the sudden news that Lefty has been found, shot dead— presumably by the "racketeers" in the union leadership. In tears, Keller exhorts the crowd to sacrifice their very lives to create "a new world." Addressing the audience, he demands, "Well, what's the answer?" The workers provide that answer-"Strike!"—in a triumphant chant that swells as the curtain falls.

Characters

Dr. Barnes

In Scene VI, Barnes is a hospital administrator torn between his convictions and his professional obligations. He deplores the ruthless, discriminatory policies of the hospital's wealthy board of directors, especially their dismissal of the talented young Dr. Benjamin; but he is also powerless to change these decisions, and sees no choice but to carry them out. Because of his advanced age, and the fact that he must provide for an invalid daughter, he feels unable to participate directly in the workers' struggle. Yet he is a passionate believer in the cause and exhorts the younger man to take up the fight he wishes he could join, encouraging Benjamin to fire a shot "for old Doc Barnes."

Dr. Benjamin

A talented and dedicated young surgeon, Dr. Benjamin learns in Scene VI that he is losing his job because of the discriminatory policies of his hospital's directors. The experience persuades him of the truth of communist theory and fires his determination to fight the capitalist system. He is tempted to emigrate to Russia, in order to work under a system of socialized medicine but decides to stay in America even though this means giving up the medical career for which his parents sacrificed so much to provide him. He takes a job as a cab driver and becomes a member of the strike committee.

Clancy

See Tom Clayton

Tom Clayton

The "labor spy" in Scene IV, "Tom Clayton" poses as a "brother" cabbie from Philadelphia. Having participated in a failed taxi strike there a few months ago, he offers that bitter experience to convince the members that a strike is useless. But a "clear voice" from the crowd—which turns out to be that of his own brother—exposes him as a strikebreaker named "Clancy," who has long been employed by industrialists to undermine militant union organizers. His charade exposed, the deceitful "Clayton" flees the wrath of the workers.

"Clear Voice" (Clancy's brother)

Unidentified at first, this "voice" emerges from the crowd in Scene IV to denounce "Tom Clayton" as a labor spy. His knowledge of "Clayton" is irrefutable, for the traitor he detests is "my own lousy brother." Like many other characters, the "voice" has discovered where his true loyalties lie; in this case, his commitment to the working class far outweighs the bonds of family.

Lefty Costello

Though he is the title character, Lefty never appears on stage; nonetheless, he is a heroic figure, in direct contrast to Fatt's villainy. A dedicated union organizer (and presumably a communist), he enjoys the confidence of the workers and seems to be their true leader, the driving force behind the strike effort. He has been elected chairman of the strike committee, and his absence at the meeting is troubling; it seems the members are counting on his leadership to stand up to Fatt and make the eagerly-awaited strike a reality.

Lefty recalls other heroic, martyred organizers of union lore, like the legendary folk-singer Joe Hill. Though their loss is deeply felt, such figures are never considered irreplaceable, for their cause is one of mass action. The play's climax comes when the workers *stop* waiting for Lefty and take responsibility for their own struggle. Though they have depended on him, they do not need a leader to give them power; they need only seize the collective power they had always had, by standing together in defiance.

Harry Fatt

Harry Fatt, the corrupt union leader, is the play's most obvious villain and the primary focus of its outrage—a stereotypical "fat cat," driven by a ruthless greed and a hunger for power. He is unmoved by the desperate poverty of the workers he claims to serve. He is purposely exaggerated, a constant force of pure evil. Odets intended the audience to see him as "an ugly menace," hovering over the lives of all the characters. Though Fatt pays lip-service to democratic principles and rails against the "anti-American" nature of communism, he is a tyrant and "racketeer," imposing his will on the union by force and intimidation. The union members overwhelmingly support a strike, and the play's political logic demands one. Yet Fatt is determined to prevent it and to maintain control by any possible means, including murder.

In his production notes, Odets leaves no doubt about the character's significance: "Fatt, of course, represents the capitalist system throughout the play." An industrialist like Fayette (in Scene II) might seem a more logical representative; but Fatt is equally a "boss" and enemy of the workers, for his corrupt leadership subverts their struggle for a better life. Whether or not he is directly employed by wealthy capitalists (and the "Labor Spy Episode" implies that he is), he serves their cause well, for his actions work as surely as theirs to secure the corrupt system. Like theirs, his power is based on the workers' continued exploitation. In Scene V, Odets emphasizes this connection by having Fatt act the role of Grady, the wealthy theatrical producer. No other character has such a dual function; the roles of "labor boss" and "business executive" are shown to be literally interchangeable. Like other bosses, Fatt can be defeated only by the collective action of the workers, who rise triumphantly against him as the curtain falls.

Fayette

The head of a large industrial corporation, Fayette is clearly in the "capitalist" camp. In Scene II, he offers his employee, the lab assistant Miller, an attractive but unsavory proposition: a generous raise and promotion if he will only agree to help develop fearsome chemical weapons and also agree to spy on his fellow scientists. Fayette is untroubled by the ethical concerns that consume Miller; his only principles seem to be profit and self-interest. "If big business went sentimental over human life," he asserts, "there wouldn't be big business of any sort!" Like other "bosses" in the play, he is an enemy of the working class. When he pays for his transgressions with a solid punch in the mouth, the audience is meant to feel that it is richly-deserved.

Florence

In Scene III, Florrie and her boyfriend Sid are tragic lovers, unable to marry because of their poverty. Their situation resembles that of Joe and Edna in Scene I; however, their scene is not a confrontation but an emotional *tableaux* (a staged depiction, often without words) of shared misery. They see that they are victims of "the money men" whose system keeps them "lonely" and "trapped"—"highly insulting us," as Florrie says. The pathos of their reluctant parting is only leavened by the suggestion that his heartbreak leads Sid to join the union cause, the only possible hope of changing their circumstances.

Florrie

See Florence

Mr. Grady

Played by the same actor that plays Harry Fatt, Grady represents the capitalist system in Scene V. He plays a wealthy theatre producer from whom Philips seeks an acting job. He is extravagantly rich, thoroughly self-indulgent, and all but blind to the suffering of others. Though he is an important part of a "creative" profession, Grady is a hard-headed businessman; he bases his decisions on economics not art. Though he has the power to relieve Philips's plight, his decision is automatic and inflexible: not even "Jesus Christ" would get a part from him if he didn't fit the type. Unable to ignore the young actor's misery, he offers a perfunctory "I'm sorry" and "good luck"—but he expresses far more concern for the health of "Boris"—his pet wolfhound.

Gunman

The Gunman is Harry Fatt's "muscle" and enforcer. Though he has few lines, he is as sinister a figure as Fatt himself, a constant menace. He "keeps order" at the union meeting by moving in to silence anyone who challenges Fatt's rule. Though the question is left open, it is possible that he (or another of Fatt's "henchmen") is Lefty's murderer. In political terms, he represents all the various forces of violence (military, police, or reactionary gangs) at the disposal of those in power. His kind is used to bully the workers into submission and crush any threat to the establishment. In the final scene, both Fatt and the Gunman try to physically restrain Agate Keller—and, significantly, are unable to do so. Keller's comrades form a human shield, protecting him as he exhorts the meeting to defiance.

Henchman

See Gunman

Irv

Irv appears briefly in Scene III, arguing with his sister Florrie over her relationship with Sid. He knows they are in love but reminds Florrie of the economic facts: Sid doesn't make enough to support her, and Florrie is needed at home, to care for their ailing mother. He adopts a stern, paternal tone (perhaps taking the role of their absent father), urging her to break off the affair and threatening Sid with violence if he persists in his attentions.

Agate Keller

Agate Keller is the last strike-committee member to address the meeting, and he leads the workers in the final call for a strike. He seems eccentric at first and deferential to the corrupt union leaders; but this turns out to be a sly pose, enabling him to criticize Fatt's regime by indirect means. As he continues, and receives the support of his comrades, his speech grows more lucid, plain-spoken, and passionate. Keller is proud to come from "deep down in the working class," and he is bitterly resentful of "the boss class," whose luxuries are paid for with the blood of workers. With growing enthusiasm, he tells the union members they have a simple choice: "slow death or fight." When Lefty's death is announced, he leads the group (and the theatre audience) into a declaration of war, exhorting the "stormbirds of the working class" to offer their lives in order to "make a new world."

Miller

A scientist working in the research department of a large industrial corporation, Miller is the "lab assistant" of Scene II and a strike-committee member. His conversion to the movement grows out of a crucial career decision. His boss, the powerful industrialist Fayette, offers him an attractive promotion and a chance to work with a renowned chemist. But the "opportunity" has several strings attached: he must sacrifice his home life, even spy on his colleague—and his job will be to develop chemical weapons, to be used in the "new war" Fayette assures him is coming. Miller has seen a brother and two cousins killed in the last war (World War I), possibly by poison gas; he is haunted by their memory and by his mother's belief that their deaths served no "good cause." His principles will not allow him to do Fayette's bidding. He refuses the job and is promptly fired. His pacifism does not prevent him, however, from punching Fayette "square in the mouth."

Edna Mitchell

In Scene I, Edna provides the motivation for her husband Joe to become active in the strike movement. Fed up with the family's desperate poverty, she bitterly vents her frustration and finally threatens to leave Joe for her old boyfriend. As she admits, her behavior is that of a "sour old nag," but Odets makes clear that this is a result of her circumstances, not her character—and that her "nagging" includes the truth Joe needs to understand what he must do. Edna loves Joe and knows that he is not to blame for their condition. She also knows, however, that their condition is truly desperate and this knowledge provokes her to consider desperate measures. When Joe finally decides to enlist in the union struggle, Edna is "triumphant" and drops all thought of breaking up the family.

Joe Mitchell

A member of the strike committee, Joe is the first to rise and speak in Lefty's place. He is not motivated by political abstractions but by the hard facts of life: the hopeless poverty that engulfs his family and the families of his fellow workers. In Scene I, he is goaded into action by his long-suffering wife, Edna. Though he works hard, they are falling further behind, and he feels powerless to change things. Edna demands that he "do something," and "get wise" to the way he and the others are being exploited. She nags, pleads, and finally threatens to leave him; at last, her desperation breaks through his denial, opening his eyes to the fact that only a strike can force the cab companies to pay a living wage. He chooses to stand and fight for his family, and that decision is what keeps his family together.

Philips

The "young actor" in Scene V, Philips becomes politicized through his inability to find a job and the intervention of Grady's communist stenographer. Devoted to his art and desperate to provide for his pregnant wife, he finds that his "market value" depends on his physical appearance, not his acting ability or his creative "soul." Under the system (represented by the wealthy, self-indulgent Grady), art must make a profit and its "creative decisions" (such as the casting of a play) are based on iron-clad business principles. Disillusioned, feeling less-than-human in his defeat, Philips is ready for the message of the Communist Manifesto and the hope of revolution. Introduced to communism by the secretary, he goes on to serve as a member of the strike committee.

Sid

The "young hack" in scene III, Sid is forced to break off his engagement to Florrie, because he cannot earn enough to support her. Humiliated and heartbroken, he feels like "a dog," not a man—for that is how he feels "the money men" treat people like him. But he can also see a day when "all the dogs like us will be down on them together—an ocean knocking them to hell and back." Though he does not speak at the meeting, he is presumably a member of the strike committee and a part of the "ocean" that rises at the play's climax.

Stenographer

In Scene V, Grady's nameless stenographer recruits the young actor Philips to the workers' cause by introducing him to communist theory. In private, she freely expresses her contempt for her boss and for all that he stands. Though she works "within the system," she is passionately committed to its eventual destruction. In anti-communist works, such subversive agents are primary villains (like the Fatt/Grady character here); they seduce their unwitting victims into ruthless service for an evil cause. But Odets's "Comrade" is humane, as her concern for Philips demonstrates. He is touched that she treats him "like a human being," and desperately in need of the nourishment she offers, both for his body (the bread her dollar will buy) and his soul (the promise of liberation). Her devotion to the cause mirrors religious fervor, and she speaks of the Communist Manifesto in biblical terms, leaving no doubt that it contains a truth that will set him free.

Themes

Class Conflict

Odets wrote *Waiting for Lefty* while a member of the Communist Party and intended it as a work of propaganda to promote the cause of a socialist revolution in America (much like the one that took place in Russia on November 6, 1917). Given that Marxist theory (based in a work called the Communist Manifesto by Karl Marx, from which leftist political philosophies derive) focuses on the economic conflict among social classes, it is perhaps inevitable that this is an intensely "class-conscious" play. Characters are clearly identified by class, and these classes are presented in vivid opposition: on the one hand, virtuous and long-suffering members of the working class; on the other, the greedy, inhumane capitalists who exploit them at every turn. Despite the realistic conventions and dialogue that characterize the domestic relationships in Scenes I ("Joe and Edna") and III ("The Young Hack and his Girl"), the larger struggle between "workers" and "capitalists" is painted in broad strokes of black and white. The villainous Harry Fatt is a purposely exaggerated stereotype, and even the heroic workers border on cartoonishness in their constant, one-dimensional nobility.

Topics for Further Study

- Compare Odets's working-class characters to the ways blue-collar workers are presented in three to four contemporary works of your own selection (sources can include movies, television, or books, as well as plays.) In your analysis, try to determine whether the differences you find are a function of: historical changes in the popular image of "the working class"; differences in the authors' intentions or beliefs; or differences of style and genre.

- Research the 1934 New York taxi strike (the incident on which *Waiting for Lefty* is based). How closely does Odets follow the historical facts? What were the consequences of the real-life strike? Considering his purposes in the play, try to determine the reasons for any changes Odets made in adapting these "current events" for his fictional production.

- Research the Communist Manifesto and outline its main arguments. Then, study the dialogue in *Waiting for Lefty* to find specific instances in which the characters advance that document's principles or echo its slogans. Write an essay that reports and analyzes your findings.

- The counterculture of the 1960s revived the notion of using drama as a means for political change in "street theatre" performances by groups like the San Francisco Mime Troupe and the staging of propaganda plays. Research this development, in newspapers and periodicals of that time. How does the radical theatre of the 1930s compare to its 1960s counterpart? In what, if any, significant ways did it change?

The effect of all this is far from subtle and may tempt modern readers to consider the work beyond all credibility. But given its specific, highly political purposes aimed at a specific moment in time, it may be unfair to evaluate *Waiting for Lefty* by traditional critical standards. Odets sought to dramatize Marxism—a notoriously dry and complex theory whose expressions are often mired in specialized jargon and clinical abstractions. Its logic is that of the "dialectic," rooted in the dynamic of competing, opposing forces (including, of course, the classes of Capital and Labor).

Odets applies Marx's insights to individual experience, replacing abstract theories with the gritty and affecting stuff of human lives. As Dr. Benjamin (played by Odets himself in some early productions) says, "you don't believe theories until they happen to you." Here the playwright shows theory happening to people as the individual characters come to realize how their misery has been engineered by the "bosses" and "money men." Individually, they are powerless to change their lot, but collectively—working as a class in response to those in power—they are able to triumph.

The wide variety of characters, and the diversity of paths they follow to the strike meeting, cuts across many traditional boundaries of class. Impoverished blue-collar workers like Joe and Sid, for example, are often considered to inhabit a different world from that of salaried, relatively-privileged professionals like Dr. Benjamin or the lab assistant Miller—yet they all belong to the strike committee, and the union is presumably stronger for the combination of their talents and backgrounds, the confluence of various classes working together.

Had Miller and Dr. Benjamin continued to serve their capitalist bosses, of course, they would have remained "class enemies" to the workers; but their experience has shown them that they are affected by the machinations of power no less than the working class; their interests cannot be separated from those of "common laborers." They have realized that their ultimate loyalty is to "the people," transcending any personal distinctions among comrades.

The diversity of "types" also increases the chances that an individual audience member will find at least one character with whom to identify—and, since each character's story points to the same, class-based enemy, it makes no practical difference which character that may be. Together, their stories demonstrate the many, insidious ways the system sustains itself and abuses those dependent upon it for their livelihood. The characters' shared determination eclipses their differences; solidarity against the capitalist class outweighs all other private loyalties, including self-interest (the prestige and money Miller turns down) and even family (the "lousy" brother Clancy who is exposed as a strikebreaker). Class struggle, according to Marx, is the primary fact of economic existence, and Odets holds to it as a central theme, though his work unfolds in a radically different form. By the time Agate Keller cries, "Well, what's the answer?," the play's logic allows only one possible response; the individual reader/viewer response to the play depends largely on our answer to another question: "Which side are you on?"

Staging

Odets specifies that *Waiting for Lefty* is enacted on "a bare stage." Whether the setting is a union hall, an office, or an apartment, there are no furnishings to help establish the scene. The full stage—extending into the audience—represents the strike meeting. For the "flashback" scenes that tell the stories of various individuals, simple lighting effects are used to create small, intimate playing spaces onstage. Such stark, relatively undefined staging is not uncommon, and "minimalist" dramatists often choose it for various aesthetic reasons. In the case of *Waiting for Lefty*, however, it is clear that Odets's intentions were not *merely* artistic. As an overtly propagandistic work of "proletarian theatre" ("proletariat" meaning the lowest class in a society), his play was meant not only for the formal, professional theatre (with its largely upper-and middle-class audience) but for any group of workers, anywhere, who wished to stage it. The simplified stagecraft thus reflects practical considerations, for it enables the work to be produced in any large meeting-hall, cheaply and with a minimum of technical sophistication.

The lack of formal scenery also tends to blur the distinction between the space of the stage and that of the audience; in effect, the entire theatre becomes the "union hall," and audience members are made to feel part of the action. The rows of seated workers facing the speaker's platform extend into rows of seated customers watching the play, and remarks from the platform are directed to both "crowds." Keller's climactic question, "Well, what's the answer?," is asked not of the workers but of the audience itself. The heckling "voices" of workers often come from actors seated within the audience, and when the "labor spy" in Scene IV is exposed, he flees off the stage and down the center aisle. Such effects are traditionally considered to make the action more vivid and immediate to the audience, to involve them on a visceral, emotional level—these goals are consistent with the play's crusading spirit. They also tend to erode the traditional distinction between drama and "real life"—sometimes to the discomfort of theatregoers who don't expect or appreciate the "invasion" of their space. *Waiting for Lefty* was not meant to be viewed with detachment, as an abstract literary fantasy, but to be experienced directly with the urgency of a real-life crisis.

None of the action takes place in a clearly enclosed space; in the personal vignettes, a spotlit area loosely defines an apartment or office, but the "outside world" of the strike meeting constantly intrudes on these private dramas. Odets directs that the "workers" onstage remain visible at the fringes of the light, milling about, often commenting directly on the action in the manner of a classical Greek chorus. Above all, the villainous figure of Harry Fatt is never absent, hovering over these small tragedies as an "ugly menace:" "Perhaps he puffs smoke into the spotted playing space," the playwright suggests in his production notes; "perhaps during the action of a playlet he might insolently walk in and around the unseeing players." In its various forms, the capitalist system he represents has brutalized each of the protagonists, but in the larger space of the strike meeting, their collective strength enables them to defy, and ultimately defeat, their oppressor. The blurring of the stage/audience "boundary" encourages a similar response to the play itself: inviting the individual viewer to feel he is a part of the collective "struggle" surrounding him and connecting the dramatized strike within the theatre to the larger, real-life drama outside. In more ways than one, Odets intended *Waiting for Lefty* as a play of the people.

Historical Context

Waiting for Lefty was inspired by a 1934 taxi strike in New York City, an event that would still have been fresh in the minds of its original, 1935 audience. But while it was sparked by a single historic incident, the play's ambitions extend much further—in fact, they reach far beyond the traditionally accepted terms of entertainment and dramatic art. Odets and his colleagues in the Group Theatre were dedicated political activists and saw their work in the theatre as the means to a much greater purpose: promoting a mass movement for a socialist revolution in America. A popular sensation in its day, the play and its politics have since fallen out of fashion—to the point that today's students may well wonder what all the fuss was about. For this reason, any attempt to appreciate Odets's achievement must be rooted in an understanding of *Waiting for Lefty*'s cultural and historical context.

The 1930s in America are remembered as "hard times" of poverty and despair, dominated by the continuing crisis of the Great Depression. Banks and businesses had failed, millions of people were without work—and, for several years following the stock market crash of 1929, the efforts of business and government leaders to manage the situation had done little to stem the tide of human suffering. The "temporary" crisis of 1929 began to appear permanent, and many Americans saw this as evidence that the country's economic and political system was intrinsically flawed: it had failed completely and could no longer be fixed by traditional remedies. In this context, political ideas that had previously seemed "radical" or "un-American" to the majority took on a new appeal. Activist movements of many kinds sprang up and enjoyed wide popularity—some resembling the right-wing fascist movements rising in Europe (particularly those found in Nazi Germany). Other movements adopted a left-wing (communist or socialist) orientation. Leftist philosophies found a particular appeal among industrial workers as well as a great many young artists and intellectuals—including Clifford Odets, who joined the American Communist Party in 1934. Though his party membership lasted only eight months, it included the period in which *Waiting for Lefty* was written.

American communists saw the Depression as bitter proof of Karl Marx's socioeconomic theories and of the betrayal of traditional American ideals. They did not consider themselves "unpatriotic" (as communists would soon be widely portrayed by the McCarthy "witch hunts" of the 1950s). Rather, by seeking power for "the people" against the power of a wealthy minority, they believed they served the true realization of patriotic ideals—which had been hijacked in the service of capital by its agents, the politicians and business leaders who were failing "the people" so completely.

The revolution Odets and his "comrades" hoped for was an American one, a quest for equality and justice. To promote its realization, they felt, was a noble and idealistic cause. The Group Theatre, then, did not produce "art of art's sake" but for the sake of the revolution. Its productions were overtly political and propagandistic—intended not to amuse but to educate and to inspire the audience to mass action. Group members did not hope to produce an evening's light entertainment or a rarefied aesthetic experience. They considered themselves above such motivations as profit for the producers or fame and fortune for the actors. They were revolutionaries, no less than soldiers on the front line, and their "weapon" was the theatre. They would harness its emotional power to spread the word and to raise the spirits of the struggling masses.

Compare & Contrast

- **1935:** The United Automobile Workers (UAW) holds its first convention in Detroit, Michigan. After a long, bitter, and often violent struggle between union organizers and corporate management, climaxed by a celebrated "sit-down" strike at a General Motors plant in Flint, Michigan, one of the nation's biggest and most important industries is unionized.

  Today: Once vilified as a subversive threat, the UAW remains one of the country's largest trade unions. After World War II, the powerful American Federation of Labor and Congress of Industrial Organizations (AFL-CIO) federation (of which the UAW was a member) removed communists and their "sympathizers" from its governing board, as the trade union movement was caught up in the rising tide of anticommunist fervor. During the post-war economic boom, while auto sales rose steadily, the UAW adopted more cooperative strategies toward management, and negotiated contracts that secured a high standard of living for a generation of autoworkers, until declining sales in the 1970s weakened the industry as a whole.

- **1935:** An Iowa statistician named George Gallup founds the American Institute of Public Opinion and develops a procedure to measure reader reaction to newspaper stories. The "Gallup Poll" initiates a new industry: the sampling and packaging of public opinion.

  Today: Polling is a pervasive part of American life, as the computer revolution has facilitated "instant" surveys and the retention of vast stores of information. Sophisticated statistical analyses play an important role in the decision-making of businesses from television networks to diaper manufacturers, who rely on polling not just to measure the preferences of customers but to anticipate their responses to products still under development. The similar use of polling by media savvy politicians and by trial attorneys injury selection has inspired wide controversy.

- **1935:** On May 11, President Roosevelt establishes the Rural Electrification Administration (REA) to facilitate the spread of electricity to sparsely populated areas. Of the thirty million Americans living in rural areas, only 10% have access to electricity. The REA not only provides valuable utilities to numerous homes, it creates numerous jobs for out of work tradesman and engineers.
  Today: Virtually all of the country has electricity. Within fifteen years of the establishment of the REA, only 10% of U.S. farms were *without* electricity. Electricity provides rural communities with access to the same technological advances as urban areas.

In *Waiting for Lefty*, Odets *dramatizes*

communist theory, translating politics to the level of the personal. The emotional "playlets" depict the effects of capitalism not in intellectual abstractions but in stark human realities, as individuals ranging from blue-collar workers to salaried professionals are each destroyed by the same, heartless "system." Each finds the same answer in mass action against the bosses. The "crowd scenes" which bring them together are staged to make audience members feel that they, too, are part of the strike meeting. Presumably, they will also be caught up in the final call to "Strike!" and feel the thrill and power of collective participation.

Odets conceived the work as "people's theatre," something closer to folk art than Broadway glamour. He designed it to be adaptable for informal performance by small, nonprofessional groups. And for several years *Waiting for Lefty was* produced as a popular fundraiser by leftist political organizations and union factions throughout the country. For Odets and his colleagues, the success of their work would not be measured in box office receipts nor critical approval but in the number of people it inspired in the struggle to transform society.

By 1935, Franklin Delano Roosevelt had been the American president for three years and his "New Deal" programs to stimulate the economy were beginning to take effect. Despite encouraging signs, the New Deal, which enacted government-sponsored work programs to put people back to work, was highly controversial. Roosevelt's conservative critics called the program communistic, while leftists felt it conceded far too much to the "evil" forces of capital.

To workers, the New Deal gave government support to the movement for industrial unionization —which had long been an arena for leftist organizers. Many saw hope in this flowering of unionism, for it seemed to be just the sort of working-class, mass action that communism advocates. However, several of the new industrial unions were tainted by charges of corruption, of dictatorial leaders, ties to organized crime, or collusion with management to limit worker's demands and prevent strikes. To communists, union corruption was a betrayal of the workers' hopes, and the amoral "labor boss" was as much an enemy of the people as the stereotyped "greedy industrialist." As the cabdrivers in *Waiting for Lefty* learn, they cannot count on leaders to give them justice—not even a heroic communist martyr like Lefty. Workers must maintain control of their own movement, and stand united to ensure that their will is carried out.

In the Cold War years following World War II, many who had been Depression-era radicals were persecuted in an anticommunist backlash through the infamous "witch-hunts" of Senator Joseph McCarthy and his supporters in the House Committee on Un-American Activities. Those in the entertainment industry were particularly vulnerable; in Hollywood, any past connection with a left-wing organization could cause one's name to appear on a privately circulated "blacklist" as an alleged "security risk." Industry executives caved in to right-wing pressure; to be blacklisted was to be unemployable and perhaps to be the subject of a congressional investigation. Those associated with causes like the Group Theatre often faced the choice of giving up their careers or compromising their principles in hopes of getting off the list. Commonly, they would be asked to swear a loyalty oath, renounce their past leftist associations, and testify freely about the activities of their colleagues.

Odets had been writing screenplays since 1941 and was called before the House Committee on Un-American Activities in 1952. He testified about his activities in the 1930s, evidently enough to satisfy the subcommittee and remove himself from further suspicion. While he didn't provide the names of anyone who hadn't already been mentioned to the committee, Odets later expressed guilt and "revulsion" over his testimony. He is said to have been tormented by the matter until his death in 1963, and he produced relatively little writing, for stage or screen, after his 1952 subcommittee appearance.

Critical Overview

Since its opening, *Waiting for Lefty* has been considered a prime example of the dramatic genre known as agitprop (and also known as revolutionary theatre and proletarian drama, among other labels). The play is often considered *the* definitive example of this genre. How one feels about that type— widely popular in its time but unfashionable in recent years—seems to have a great deal to do with one's critical reaction.

Waiting for Lefty's original production in 1935 was a critical success and a popular hit. Reviewing it for the *New York Times*, Brooks Atkinson praised it as not only "one of the best working-class dramas that have been written" but as "one of the most dynamic dramas of the year in any department of our theatre." He stressed its realism and intensity: "the characters are right off the city pavements; the emotions are tender and raw, and some of them are bitter." Remaining neutral on the play's political message, Atkinson stressed its social importance as well as its relevance to the troubled moment in history it portrays: "People who want to understand the times through which they are living," he wrote, "can scarcely afford to ignore it." Harold Clurman, a founder of the Group Theatre, recalled of an early performance that the audience joined spontaneously and enthusiastically in the climactic call to "Strike! Strike!" As he recalled in *The Fervent Years: The Story of the Group Theatre and the Thirties*,

Clurman considered their reaction both "a tribute to the play's effectiveness" and "a testimony of the audience's hunger for constructive social action. It was the birth cry of the thirties. Our youth had found its voice." By July of 1935 (within six months of its debut), *Waiting for Lefty* had been produced in thirty cities across the country. For several years, productions of the play were staged as fundraisers and morale boosters by a variety of left-wing organizations.

While he produced one of its most celebrated works, Odets wrote little else in the agitprop vein. His later dramas and screenplays are far more conventional, with little emphasis on overt political messages. For this reason—coupled with his commercial success on Broadway and in Hollywood—many of his revolutionary comrades accused him of selling out the cause and betraying his principles. Odets clearly changed his thinking in some ways and came to renounce his Communist Party membership. Other critics, however, question whether he experienced any abrupt reversal in his earlier conceptions of drama. In this view, *Waiting for Lefty* is a one-of-a-kind effort, produced in a burst of idealistic exuberance, and its political crusading is atypical of Odets's usual concerns, before and after its composition. As a whole, his writing bears more resemblance to this play's intimate domestic sketches than to the high drama of the raucous strike meeting. In such works as *Awake and Sing!*, *Golden Boy*, and *The Big Knife*, Odets's strengths are generally considered to include his realistic characterization and dialogue as well as his deft exploration of personal and domestic conflicts.

Waiting for Lefty was not written "for the ages," to stand as an immortal work of art but for a specific time and culture to advance particular social and political aspirations. In that light, it may be somewhat irrelevant that, by most accounts, the play no longer inspires the admiration and enthusiasm it sparked in the 1930s. To modern tastes, it typically appears as an anachronism, obsolete in both style and substance. Its slogan laced dialogue seems forced and unnatural, while its broad characterizations seem simplistic and melodramatic. Its moralizing tone is far less palatable today, when preaching of any kind is unfashionable, and its "party-line" analysis seems dogmatic and unsophisticated.

Most importantly, the solution it offers—a communist revolution—appears in a radically different light for modern audiences. During the Depression, it appeared as a viable and desirable alternative; true believers thought they could glimpse it on the horizon. But after decades of tense Cold War geopolitics followed by the rapid decline of world communism in the late-1980s, to even consider such a revolution *possible* requires an imaginative leap. It is certainly possible to appreciate a work for its formal qualities, or its treatment of universal human themes, apart from its specific "message" and historical context—but for a play like *Waiting for Lefty*, the message was its entire reason for being, and its ability to influence audiences in that crucial moment of history was its greatest measure of success.

What Do I Read Next?

- Odets's other works provide for interesting comparisons with *Waiting for Lefty* and reveal the full range of his talents and concerns. Two works from his time with the Group Theatre, *Awake and Sing!* (1935) and *Paradise Lost* (1935), each make political points by relating the story of an American family but they do so in very different ways. *Awake and Sing!* is a realistic account of the struggles of a working-class Jewish family, akin to the domestic vignettes in *Waiting for Lefty*. *Paradise Lost* concerns a declining middle-class family and relies heavily on symbolism, with each family member representing a particular middle-class value.

- *The Big Knife*, written by Odets in 1949, deals with the personal and professional conflicts of a movie actor named Charlie Castles, who ultimately commits suicide. It can be seen as a reflection of the difficulties Odets encountered while working for Hollywood and might even be said to foreshadow the turmoil he would experience during the McCarthy era.

- Odets's contemporaries in Depression-era political drama provoke insightful comparison. John Howard Lawson's *Marching Song* details the conflict between a union and a gang of vicious strikebreakers; *Black Pit*, by Albert Maltz, concerns the struggles of a group of West Virginia coal miners. While their themes and goals closely resemble those of *Waiting for Lefty*, each play has its own, unique voice—an indication of the wide spectrum of participants and philosophies within the radical theatre movement.

- *Hard Times*, by Studs Terkel (1970) is a rich oral history of the Depression, culled from hundreds of interviews with people from all walks of life. Their first-hand accounts combine to paint a vivid picture of those times, with an intensity seldom found in traditional historical accounts.

Sources

Atkinson, Brooks. Review of *Waiting for Lefty* in the *New York Times*, March 27, 1935.

Clurman, Harold. *The Fervent Years: The Story of the Group Theatre and the Thirties*, Knopf, 1945, reprinted, Harcourt, 1975.

Further Reading

Brenman-Gibson, Margaret. *Clifford Odets, American Playwright: The Years from 1906 to 1940*, Atheneum, 1982.

> This is an extensive, thoroughly researched account of Odets's early career, and contains a detailed treatment of his years with the Group Theatre.

Goldstein, Malcolm. *The Political Stage: American Drama and Theatre of the Great Depression*, Oxford, 1974.

> Goldstein presents a full history of Depression-era political drama, covering not only the Group Theatre but many similar organizations, including the Theatre Guild, Theatre Union, and the "Living Newspaper" productions of the Federal Theatre Project.

Goodman, Walter. *The Committee: The Extraordinary Career of the House Committee on Un-American Activities*, Farrar, Strauss & Giroux, 1968.

> Goodman offers a thorough history of the Congressional committee that was at the center of the Cold War anticommunist crusade, including the

appearances of Odets and several of his 1930s contemporaries.

Mendelsohn, Michael J. *Clifford Odets: Humanitarian Dramatist*, Everett/Edwards, 1969.

> Mendelsohn provides a concise biography of the playwright, including a critical analysis of each of his works.

Smiley, Sam. *The Drama of Attack: Didactic Plays of the American Depression*, University of Missouri Press, 1972.

> This work of literary scholarship closely analyzes a wide range of politically concerned plays of the 1930s, including works by Odets, John Howard Lawson, George Sklar, Albert Maltz, Paul Perkins, and Elmer Rice.